TRAJECTORIES

JEFF O'BRIEN

Fieldstone Press
NEW LEXINGTON   KINGWOOD

Also by Jeff O'Brien

PROSE

Seasons in Upper Turkeyfoot: A Countryman's Journal

Fieldstone Press
522 Handwerk Road
Markleton, PA 15551

Copyright 2000 by Jeff O'Brien
All rights reserved
Manufactured in the United States of America
Printed on acid-free paper

Library of Congress Cataloging-in-Publication Data

O'Brien, Jeff, 1945-
    Trajectories: poems / by Jeff O'Brien
        p. cm.
ISBN 0-9702801-0-6
    I. Title

Library of Congress Card Number 00-105465

Grateful acknowledgement is made to the following publications in whose pages some of these poems first appeared: English Journal, The Loyalhanna Review, Many Mountains Moving, Pif Magazine, The Pittsburgh Post-Gazette, The Pittsburgh Quarterly, The Southern Poetry Review, yawp.

For
ELSIE
and her daughters
MILDRED, AILEEN, MARGERY, and LINDA

Give me the world if Thou wilt,
but grant me an asylum for my affections.
TULKA

CONTENTS

I

Pump Two Is On 3
Wrecking Bar 4
Confession in Late March 5
Bathers 6
Holy Days With Little Leaguers 7
Courage, Sister 9
Yang's Pond 10
Saving a Marriage 11
Deeper in the Country 12
Firewood 13
A Sonneteer Has a Change of Heart 14
The Point 15
Blame Wind 16
Contemplating Suicide 17
Workshop Buddhas 18
Hills Between Us 19
Dogs and Poets in Paradise 20

II

After Each Stanza, a Barn 23
Stonepile 24
Clouds End Drought 25
Breathing at St. Michael's 26
Infestation 27
Laurel Mountain Psalm 28
Holsteins 29
Orchard Pond 30
August 31

Fade *32*
Assault *35*
Not Geoffrey *36*
Twelfth Sign *37*
Hammock *39*
Pike Town *40*
Basic Oxygen Furnace *41*
Coffee in North Apollo *42*
This Private Property *43*
Retinoscopy *44*

III

Snake Killer *47*
Many *48*
Songbirds *49*
Collaborators *50*
Murrow's Common Prayer *51*
Fat *53*
Meetings in Hoarfrost *54*
Interlude *55*
IV *55*
Trajectories *56*
Coronary *58*
The Settled Life *59*
The Renderer Faces Surgery *60*
Proof *61*
Last Reading in Pittsburgh *62*
Five-Point *63*
Believers *64*
Resurrection *65*

NOTES 67

I

Pump Two Is On

You found me again
after the summer of nines
after the equinox
when the high cold air
lowers with the sun
and fills the swales and shadows
and I wear Polartec to the Kwik Stop
for milk and gasoline and cash
and through spun polyester felt
the warmth of your small hand
against my arm and all
those extravagant sensations
fall through me again
the tannin and the areolae
the tea hot in your mouth
receipt a slip of tongue
forgotten in the ATM
and now my neighbors with their fingers
cold in their jug handles
know my balance.

Wrecking Bar

The house is empty, and the rooms are quiet.

We know each other well, the house and I,
Chestnut kerfed before the blight.
So many forms have we embraced
And stripped, swinging the wrecking bar,
Splinters flying in the ringing steel.

See how the hammer fits my hand, a hollow
In the grip worn by my thumb?
Behold the floors' exploded views!
I do this any time I please,
Eurythmic in my La-Z-Boy,

I own the will
To float the shingles off the roof,
To free the nails and launch them
Into constellations arched
Across my space as dull as zinc.

Ceilings open, plaster drifts,
Romex waves in currents of the night.
I climb inside her walls and with a twist
Vault through her joists and leave
The Dipper spinning on its handle from my flight.

This is not the way the others left.

Confession in Late March

Sure of snow,
we stand
in empty woods,
looking up
into the mist,

Careless, wet.
What holds
it heavy here,
sky domes twigged
and spined with hills,

Hemispheres
of this,
this hanging day,
tiny you,
inverted, gesturing,

Word made cloud
before
your hot red mouth,
solitude
too fine for speech?

Bathers
(Neshannock Falls, Pennsylvania, July 4, 1918)

Crayfish hunt the rock shade
where my people crossed,
nine generations in the creek
planked bank-to-bank at Walker's Mills,
chestnut squared by adze and trussed,
water striders rowing in the lees,
summer stretching out its legs,
glimmer spinning on the underpinnings.

Girls pose on flat stones below the falls,
waiting, bonnets and black hose,
waiting at the edge of womanhood,
sun bands bright above the water line,
the dam still holding at their backs,
fresh husbands still in France,
dreams they scarcely knew.
        The creek runs cold.

These eyes, these dark eyes dead,
and no one left to cross,
the bridge abandoned suffers rain,
the road improved,
the rutted mud, the horse smell gone,
the mill, the millpond gone,
the barns, the schoolhouse gone,
the steel span engineered,

Volvos keen across the girdered grid,
Crayfish vanishing backwards
in drifting volleys of slough.

Holy Day With Little Leaguers

The workmen get drunk early and steer home.

Snow survives in furrows
in the cornfields against town,
the sun a far-off freight,
an echo of the year is all that's left,
rolling up the tracks from Bando Station.

The waitress in the Silk Lamp dimpled says
she's forbidden in the kitchen to bait traps,
all the snapping's sure to frighten off the clientele,
it's the way she says it doe-eyed, cli-in-tell,
it's the way she says I've surely heard 'bout her and Lloyd.

The establishments I frequent feature women with their
      babies on the side.

The part-time cop beneath the heater nods
noble as a shortstop should be, calls me coach
when I walk in hungry on this eve of eves,
I've been around too long, it's true
she'll get no money if her husband sits in jail,

The moon across the street at perigee,
a caution on the empty feedstore glass,
the welded tinsel stars we've always known
swinging in the grit that blows down Main,
each of us alone.

Specials of the Day include: Court-ordered visitations,
      PFAs.

She'll work two jobs, she imps, she'll be okay,
she's young enough to think so anyway and I
dip jalapeno poppers, bless beer-battered fries,
think a hope for Lloyd who rode the bench,
his money in his shoe, waiting in his F-150 now,
his turn in the dark soon due, and for the boards
beneath our soles lest we fall through,
chewed by rats up from the frozen river.

Courage, Sister

Rain again upon the pond,
circles spreading, intersecting,
leaping silver and collapsing,
clouds roll over her in tides,
swells intuent over bars,
mumming thunder ever present,
boozing husband overdue,
welcome as an end to waiting,
more rain coming and she stays,
hears it driving up the valley,
swallows high in legs of rain
flying stunts above the field,
feeding in the walking storm.

When cardinals sing like drunks she knows
the rain will ease, and corridors of sky
will brighten the ticking, bibulous earth;
hummingbirds at dripping lilacs
whirl their blurred infinities.

Calming now to polished jade,
the pond reflects red-wings
preening in the hickory,
bobbing on the ripples
from the snake that hunts the reeds,
black tongue lashing,
mayflies caught in surface tension,
spotted newts suspended just below,
wagging their transparent tails,
charging after what she has a guess,
the next, cold drops of rain again begin
to raise the rings upon her flesh,
the unrelenting spring.

Yang's Pond

Throbs obsidian
and periscoped with bullfrogs
watching us;
          cattails flank the sun in ruin.

Urge that braids the gnats
in helix flings the bat
though dunning air;
          cattails ring the pond in ruin.

Pulse beneath the planks
that pulls us through the fluid night
between two moons,
          cattails hoary and in ruin,

Joins us on the stair,
as when between our limbs
we swim the same,
          words and pain the same.

Saving a Marriage

Screen in the screen door,
menthol pouring over us
unbraiding on the braided rug.

Fire gallops in the grate,
hot against our soles, a nice effect,
embers in Ember days.

Back in town with no cable
you called, old enough to be alone
(daughters have their dramas to construe)

Young enough to be consoled
by sex without regret;
weeping slickens flesh.

Crows announced you in the wood.
Leave the door open you said,
spreading out the finch feathers

You found under the molting limb;
I touched a match to The Review,
and all I thought of was your mouth.

Leaving was the wise thing, yet what's left?
April's high rills bend the trees,
fine bones clatter in their crowns,

Cherries shoot their tender wings,
bits of bark embedded in our skin,
wind steps through the screen.

I think perhaps we will survive,
and wouldn't that be something
in a flurry of gold quills?

Fire stumbles in the grate against iron doors.
You'll be okay. I'll be okay.
Not we.

Deeper in the Country

Through bare maples tossing in the thaw
rain clouds soak up light from the resorts
stainless on the ridge beyond the fields,
manure spread, the stubble sopping.

Yardlights fling their amber quills above the barns.
Farmers' sons in blocked-up trailers
jack their boots inside their dripping panes
wet with boiling anything but beef.

Door chain slaps against the glass. They eat.
From the soiled hollow of their couch
they watch epiphanous TV, all
the pretty explosions, and there they sleep,
the smell of milk forever in their clothes.

Firewood

Oblivious to men in coveralls
heaving rolls of snowfence
into the dumptruck bluebirds
twitch with home.

I would sleep with the dogs on their sides
in the sun, haul away, whistling.

The male turns in the nest hole
complementing breast-to-tail
the female riding in pastel a bramble
making her decision.

I let drop the chainsaw on crushed grass,
hands ringing in concussive quell.

Under the rusting logshed roof
I stack a childhood of summers,
sheet iron banging in the breeze,
nothing left but sunlight in the yard,

punctured sod, a hundred little sawdust
heaps where limbs fell hard.

When bluebirds end and township men begin
again to hammer stakes into the ground,
I'll have a week of heat, or maybe two.
Heartwood burns the slowest.

I accomplished this in an afternoon.
I am 53. I ache.

A Sonneteer Has a Change of Heart

Your scenery killed me in the end.
What did you expect?
You can stop searching now.
No need to find the sonnet
that I sent -- as if
you had to look.

The asking maybe spooked you,
polite and sane, a sensible request
to *antelope.edu* where you strive aloof,
pedantic, grubbing intellect,
as if you ever had to.
All I wanted was to learn

The limit of my flight,
to measure speed and altitude,
that I may never drink again at sunset
Wild Turkey from the bottleneck by fire,
nor watch my shadow cross the Little Sandy,
tangled up in sage and rabbit brush,

Nor trust in love, nor want to.

The Point

We reach The Point
             not far,
where the land falls away,
and we lie above the valley
breathless and singular
in binocular fusion,
brinkmen among clouds.

Farmer on the far slope,
stick shout and rubber boots,
calls his Jerseys up the path,
straggle of udders swinging,
bone holcads towed to parlor,
tranced animal following
all we remember of migration.

Spider filaments unreel
toward the ridges blue with wind,
thistle seed takes flight,
bursts of floss above the trees
sloughing in the creases,
hawk below us chased by crows,
the whole lecherous earth
gone off and left us here,
waiting for a stronger gust,
wanderers, still.

Blame Wind

Crows drop one wing
and launch to wail
above the roaring wood,
the wind pulls off
our clothes, we could
blame the waning shards
of sundown in the pine,
or undiluted swans
in liquid weaving line
whiter than the clouds
and webbed contrails,
or wet stropped moon
and all the violet between
the hawk that cups
the dusk under its wings
and you, the pine spire,
or the moon alone.

Contemplating Suicide

Our conclusions are wrong.
Take this storm, for instance, out
of the northeast, unsettling, the wind
invading hollows we thought
safe, buzzing under the brass weather
stripping, lifting the vents, turning the sticky
fan blades backward
in the kitchen.

Juncos congregate in the broken
birch where water hangs
among the catkins and the veins, the house,
the yard, the barn, inverted in each drop,
birds as duochrome as February,
waiting to be fed, children
waiting, leaving
us no choice.

Immersed in fog
dissembling we
celebrate mortality.

Workshop Buddhas
(for Jerry)

Syllables lie limp
between the shining elbows.

Workshop Buddhas,
noggins brindled from the sun,
nostrils flared among the long bones
of the women
and the tan girls,
desperate to salvage
art from urge,
look to Vera,
slack with sense beneath her bun.

Vera claims her mind's a blank
and fans herself with imagists.
For the flaccid, it just comes.

Hills Between Us

Driving the one distance
rooted in the hollows
of our throats,
the hills unfurl
as separate trees
each crowned with its own light.

How many entrances
and exits, in the thousands
of stacked stones,
how many paths,
how many summers
turned to fall
across the one road lengthening?

The long, low light between us,
the grass that gives the wind
a face, the trees
that give it voice,
the satin necks of horses
perfectly aligned,
all of it, the absence,
will outlive us.

The birds that flash as one,
the leaves that lift
before the rain, the bolt
of sunset settling the hills,
the one hard road between us
begs me back,
begs me stay;
the moon travels one way,
clouds another.

Dogs and Poets in Paradise

Even a dying man will comment
on the sundown or another bloom,
if he be lucky lying conscious on the ground.

Even poets out late with the dogs,
pear tree overarching frost and heavy stars,
think up clauses on the brittle grass.

Sing in tremolo of middle age,
bad marriages, abandonments, the knife,
made to warble on the page like screech owls in the
    wood.

How long will the money last, how long,
as smoke rolls powder blue off of the roof,
how far away this paradise of dogs from ruin?

Who will spend good money for old words,
meteors and comets and puddings for sale,
ahs ascending into heaven and The Library of Congress?

A rounder view is common among dogs,
dying is their business; poets sigh and juggle woes,
making art from art, though *people must have puddings.*

II

After Each Stanza, a Barn

Stories string out in the darkness
down the two-lane south from town.
Houses face the black macadam,
country people in their kitchens

Bless the steaming mashed potatoes,
praising Jesus in the twilight
behind porch posts, in their windows
glowing yellow, thank the Lord.

What they won't say crouches outside
in the night fields, in the hollows,
where their hopes lie disconnected
between farms and rising silos.

Here a woman curses cancer
for the men who lay before her.
Here another keeps a light on
as a warning to the hated.

Here a man led off in handcuffs
for the bones cracked in his trashpile.
Dogs and neighbors breathed her burning.
Bolt the door and load the gun.

No prayers answered down the hard road,
no epiphanies in waiting,
but the winter and the young moon
keeping pace,

Blade keen.

Stonepile

The jolt they felt behind the plow,
the oxen and the doubletree,
the dead boys and the men broken
who cleaned these fields,
who heaved these stones,
the black dirt in their wounds,
their savaged hands
they haul me down
through sloughing limbs,
through ragged moss,
in lichened rooms they hang
my bones on hammered chains
until I too am land.

Clouds End Drought
(after Po Chu-I)

Facing hemlocks I planted
along Handwerk Road to break
the wind near the garage I come to harmonies
of thunderstorms and the hint
of isolate mystery.

Rain darkens gravel and dust,
trees sway hips and rub
shadowed thighs together bowing silver
to the four directions,
heart gone blank and white as sky,

Alone with the katydid that blew
through the open doorway to alight
on my bare leg -- we touched as lightly once,
stroke of long antennae,
smell of wet stones.

Blades of wind-rinsed lilies
toss before black hemlocks,
body idle, mind adrift, hardly human
any more and grateful for it,
emptiness our nature.

Breathing at St. Michael's

Consecrate
your perfect
                tense
enrapt in clapboards and the dazzled trees
overreaching in the stagy breeze
reading here in Rector
                stop
reconsider if you please your splendid self
doubt your own sweet easy thought
listen for the crickets in the weeds
watch our tidal air fill up the sky
stretch the moment
                taut
and lung-to-lung
we'll breathe each other's fear.

Infestation

In the path of the tornado
a welder home from night
turn falls asleep and drops Macbeth
onto the shag, ambition
overvaulting in six twelves.
                    Harpier cries -- 'tis time.

Torch incensed the beetles mass
on windows, working hard
and thriving in America,
stacked like cordwood
in the sheds of Pennsylvania,
                      hulls piled up beneath the lamp.

Cornered at his eye a beetle drinks,
weird sisters spin the trees
out of the ground, grace
and renown in blisters broken
weeping on his arms,
                      no man master of his time.

Laurel Mountain Psalm

I unroll my mat
I lie in trembling blades

I open my knife
I cast peels into the gorge

I break flesh in my teeth
I swallow multiplying juices

I fold my coat beneath a sheet of wind,
This valley and the space above, my opus.

One stripped stem
Of timothy awakens

Singing anapaests
Whistling dactyls

Whoever listens
Finishes a poem in his sleep.

Holsteins

Holsteins saw us.
flat heads lifting,
We heard the grass
rip from the root,
bots aswarm in perfect stares.

Why tell?
What Latinate
to phrase the taste
of salt, what stems
tongue that hollows out the block?

Spoken, will you
never loll again
where we all feed,
and I lower
to green dreams in green shade,

Flying off to find you in the oaks,
and nothing yet?

Orchard Pond

Flesh flies
scrape wings
on fallen plums,
mid-day sun
a stab in amber
where masked wasps
chew at wounds.

Carefully,
come to me,
crushing,
just once.

Hot stones,
old water,
guide my hand
across ripe skin

As the snails rise
blooming viscid
tail to horn
on spiral keels,

Sums
of middle densities,
one molecule
between the lips.

None of this
is far
beyond what ruins us:
muscle,
ferment,
appetite,
as leaves erode.

August

This is merely happiness.

Witness to my own events
I see the sun rise as I sleep,
hear the river thin and quick
through wooded crowding hills,
smell the curling corn in tassel,
feel the shadows on my back
of blackbirds passing,
escadrilles that perforate
the ground.

I have no one to save.

Fade

I.

No comet fright this spring.
No omen. No deluding flares
through Ursa Major, no Big Dipper
guillotined by superstition,
which is what we call belief and laugh.

Hyakutake,
seen through torn and racing clouds,
blue gasps of adrenal rush,
missed us, *sayanora*, thumb to nose.
Plant beans.

Hale-Bopp passed with two thick tails,
close enough to kill.
Even cynics like you and me, leaning
on our hoes, saw incinerating trees,
felt tectonic shuddering.

A team of dreamers danced their way
into the void, Nikes on in bed,
waiting for the calvary, a ride, tranquilized
and drunk, plastic on their heads.
Well, we hope it worked.

No comet fright this spring.
No latent joy. No clashes with infinitude.
Apparition takes its time.

How desperate our needs. How vain
to think we are worth saving.
Chop weeds.

II.

We regret that we are unable
to use the enclosed material.
Thank you for giving us the
opportunity to consider it.
                         The Editors.

III.

No comet fright this spring.
No latent bliss. Nothing.
Cynics lean upon their hoes,
Open and exposed,
while
Dreamers join the wistful dead,
Sneakers on in bed.

No comet fright this spring.
No future tense. Nothing.
Tillers of the earth, the book,
Never stop to look,
while
Apparition, mute as time,
Parables in mime.

No comet fright this spring.
Nothing.

IV.

We regret,
thank you for giving.
                        The Editors.

V.

No April apparition.
Planters of the cold wet ground,
place your faith in seed;
and give a moment's silence, please,
for the vainglorious dead.
No comet fright this spring.
No present tense.
No Thing.

Assault

I disenjoy poetry.
Among the overly polite, the small,
scattered through the musty hall, clad black,
I shift from haunch to haunch and hear him read,
he lisps sing-song into the mike, his guts exposed
and I conclude: Poets I dislike.

In those cloy tones that poets use, the small
epiphanies he croons, as women with their necks exposed
hum to splanchnic currents only poetry
excite when sung by thoughtful men in black,
rumpled, and their ties tucked in -- poets I dislike
engorged by their own words they love to read.

I hate his shamelessness, his sex exposed,
as if he were the first to screw, this poet I dislike,
I hate his preciousness and fight the urge to raise a small
but vivid crater on his gibbous moon, to strike a blow for
    poetry,
for all the rest of us who have unpublished words to read
and long to make the down-necked women hum, to pose
    in black.

Small consolation, 'tis agreed, to thump a lumpen poet I
    dislike,
but he says "poim" and vast caverns of dim poetry flash
    black.
Envy haunts the increate and stalks the few who read, the
    baggy-kneed, exposed.

Not Geoffrey

Good Christ, the wine country is crawling with O'Briens!
You blame the academic track for your mistake,
derailed, retrieved, and lost again on the Pacific
Rim in Nichols Hall, then off to bars for fiction hires,
gruesome work what stirs the recreative sylphs.

In pressed cold Appalachian fields,
rotting grass spots black, and I,
mistaken for a younger mind, ferment.

Maceration is no way to spend the night.

Twelfth Sign

I control the coast,
willing the hurricane to the cities,
clearing the beaches
of pressure-treated decks,
another disaster declared,
another shout from me,
high over the Atlantic
in the stationary orbit
of my converted bedroom.

I shut down.
Save yourself.
First the deluge,
then the drought.

Water slaps on stones,
under the back porch gutter
fifty-five gallons of storm
brim in the Rubbermaid drum,
four feet of rain in a pillar,

     and a fish,

thin bluegill spirit   oh goddamn,
waving her fins suspended
just under the common plain,
scowling through the reflection,
clouds adrift between realms.

Long we stare, and long
I sense a stronger will,
a Greater Elegance.

Fresh out of explanations,
I have asked enough questions
of heaven for one life.
In the night mansion of Jupiter
I bow to the Ganoids,
I pray to the Teleosts.

I control nothing.
Helpless in a sieve
she sprays my face,
wounds my thumb and finger
with her rays, convulsing
in the insubstantial air.
I cast ablutions in the main,
departure and return
one motion.

Hammock

Swing in that between
between the dusk and night before
before the cloud pillars expire,
blue in moonless blue,

Swing in that between
between to watch the dark lie down
lie down in dry fists of the fields,
crickets keening light,

Engines shouting down
the geese in dark procession down,
the vires black-beaked in the boughs
swing in that between.

Pike Town
(for the strikers and their families)

This could be any red
and yellow Turnpike town
stripped clean of goldenrod
and bearded with motels,
good land zoned and slapped by rain,
for sale up to the graves.

Except for the high ground,
the ruthless pillared manse
of Zimmerman the King,
birner of cattle and immigrants,
newborns cold as tourists
in the tents outside Jerome.

Except for the high ground,
county sandstone courthouse
where progress is ordained,
Country Club complete
and Harding due, mild
terror in the coalfields of 1922.

Young woman, tear your hair,
wrap your child in canvas,
no one cares, sleepers
tiered in the motor drone.
Where there's money to be mined
we'll pave the bloody ground.

Basic Oxygen Furnace

The grinding void of the mill inside
the thud of age I never got over
the groan of tonnage not from the first day
everything black and about to incinerate
or crush me leaving only hardhat
goggles metatarsals car payment
the smudge of a silverfish expendable
at risk an ancient arrangement.

Mike Micklo punched in already sour
as a goat in salty Carharts bloated
at The Millgate from tomato juice and beer
and porch sleep locked out by his crazy
wife who gave the boy a hammer rude
awakening child born late in life
a blessing to Stern's evil Mellons
and to that bastard Edgar Speers
and his world production record.

Graphite rained three times a shift
on men in the BOF kerchiefs
tied around their jaws shoulders
heaped with glitter vessel tipped
ladle brimmed with steel stopper burst
molten splatter tracers burned through bone
asshole craneman on incentive
company man high in the carbon cloud
ran the length of Sheol filling molds.

We saved ourselves behind a beam
shaking in each others arms

My wife should see Mike Micklo yelled
in the clang and fire and the shudder
Story for the kids he stank yelling
the ones who move away and don't
come back except in your sleep
nothing left but a carbon smear.

Coffee in North Apollo

"Oh, Donna" spins in the Yakkitty-Yak,
tonic for old teenagers,
not brave, just bored by portent,
the Kiski River at their backs.

Beneath a sky as grey as slag,
the river runs ignored, past the oxide
corrugations seen through trees
aflutter with high-water plastic bags.

Elbows countered pale where elbows go,
they raise their heavy coffee mugs,
toast themselves in fluted stainless,
distortions they no longer know.

Steel remains their medium.
Sudden death or healing -- where are they?
Here, they'll take it either way.
Kiskiminetas, brown tedium.

This Private Property
(for Daniel Groff, 65, who died by his own hand, March 28, 1999)

We have some time, some time
to talk, besides, the Sheriff
doesn't start 'til nine, turn up a cinder block,
the cosmos teems with systems, does it not?

Featherweight my pretty Ithaca
cradled in my arm, be not alarmed,
we have some time, some time,
two-hundred billion suns in just the Milky Way!

You'd think beneath these tender leaves
and streaming wind that stack
the coins of daylight at our feet,
you'd think an alchemist could live alone.

But no, but no, solicitors
with front end loaders come,
the barbered, bandoleered,
the tie-tacked come
to Furnace Hill where Groff
with old refrigerator parts
did make it snow!

Bread is made for laughter,
and wine gladdens life,
and money answers everything,
the Bible tells me so.

Retinoscopy

Sunset powders all the borderland,
bronze rubbed across the rim of day
welded to the tossing hills by ribbed red sun;
color siphons in the west,
cooling circles and ellipses,
thousand-noted mysteries,
deep in the penumbra of the earth rolled back.

Through the seam of day and night
the lords of animus proceed
left and right upon the gravel road,
smooth riders in a rush, Broncos, Blazers, Cherokees,
chimeras trailing yellow dust,
numb to their pneumatic passing.

In the valley of impenetrable mist,
guns and engines violate the dusk.
Amid the green tribes of the hill, you
are left to hear the trill, and this as good
a time as any to go blind.

III

Snake Killer

Throat deep crimson at the blade,
What's another garter more or less?
The envelope I dropped and raised the spade,
The Committee wishes me success.

What's another garter more or less?
The dusty scales, the sunset eyes;
The Committee wishes me success,
Quick to draw the beetles and the flies.

The dusty scales, the sunset eyes,
Reptiles seem the quickest to degrade,
Quick to draw the beetles and the flies,
Lashing at the blade.

Reptiles seem the quickest to degrade,
The common heart is emptying the well;
Lashing at the blade,
Beyond regret, what is left to tell?

The common heart is emptying the well,
The longer length crawls headless in the grass;
Beyond regret, what is left to tell?
Heaven bruised where the sun falls fast.

The longer length crawls headless in the grass,
I dropped the envelope and raised the spade,
Bruised heaven where the sun falls fast,
Throat deep crimson shade.

Many

Ten million stipulations
wound the winter woods;
numbers go against us.

Too many dreams drift to our hips,
too many poets making notes
steaming in too many clothes
behind their little ponies,
too many servers, towers, beeves;
six billion is too many to believe that keloid
fades in heaven.

Lie with me in warm deep snow,
we'll touch each other's scars;
one beech leaf trembles in one wind,
one ribbed membrane apostrophe
completing our contraction.

Songbirds

Not even in Ohio
can poor James Wright find print
not even decades dead
which is relief
and agony
for me, yodeling like a cardinal
to get the evening right.

How do I write the budding hills,
April bleeding in their crowns?
What do I say about the creek
in flight, the valley bruming
cheek to rim, dissolving
the last ridge in indigo?
Why not plagiarize
the doves' refrain deep
in hemlock pyramids of night?

What a fool,
fool, fool.

How absurd this two-note singing,
fledging and rejecting.
Irruption thank you never
meets their present needs.
I save them all, starlings
flocking on the wall.
Well then, send back these...

Consolation I expected in return
of Wright, Carruth, and Strand,
a laugh to see the potent thumbed,

editors benumbed as thugs
from thousands of submissions,
-- what it is
is damned discouraging.

Purblind babblers,
birds and me,
shrug in our roosts.
Evening in the valley we hear trains,
our slope of earth atremble with their weight.
This is a song we know.
Tomorrow rain.

Collaborators

She, born in Bulgaria and raised
in Newark, has spent time
as an editor, journalist,
and puppet-costume maker.

He, born in Cambridge and raised
in Belize, has spent time
as a folk-singer, poetry critic,
and migrant farm worker.

They live in Jackson and Key West,
sometimes together.
Of course they teach,
languishing.

Murrow's Common Prayer
(Spring in Germany, 1945)

I am the least
important person here.

This is no time to talk
of the surface,
switch off the monitor.

We have left undone
those things
which we ought to have done.

The powerless pull
small belongings
on anything with wheels.

We have done
those things
we ought not to have done.

There is no desperation,
tanks turn
the corner, wounded spill.

We have too much
followed the devices
of our hearts.

Down in the air raid
shelter money
dirty ankle deep

Has no meaning,
the war
more real than peace.

People have little
to say,
there are no words.

Fat

A sentence flies in the sour-milk wind that blows up
    Parson's Run,
"I'll take it Super-Sized," spoken in the idiom of the
    American herd,
and something under the dull circle of the sun on sterile
    water,
something under the troweled creekbed licks its chops.

The stream jumps along forgotten under roads, the butter
    plant manager
knows it's there, one boot on the yellow railing at the
    edge of the parking lot,
enjoying a smoke, suspicious of strangers, watching
    children watching sparrows
through McDonald's fuscia bars, come for all they can
    swallow.

Water clear as solvent bobbles along the drain pipe maw
under the soft-fleshed thousands in their radiant cars
    intersecting.
O! This is a glorious day over ninety-nine billion sold.
O! This is a powerful nation under the carbon flag
    snapping,

A procession of meat from horizon to horizon, beautiful
to what eats the water clear, a wilderness pristine
to what comes next, beatified at the dawn of time,
famished.

Meetings in Hoarfrost

I.

Winter takes the field,
crystal cliffs and balustrades
build in clear midnight,
pooling starlight leading us
to expect more meteors.

II.

Beyond human space,
spirants of the boreal,
galaxies aground,
our breath rises in one braid,
bodies consonant in rime.

Interlude

Gravity alone,
a mere celestial spinning,
holds you in the air,
centripetal adagio.
You weigh nothing in my hands.

IV

In waxed shoes I step
through wet grass bent with leaving.
Cancer blooms like violets,
your blood drawn in tubes,
peach trees blossom in cold light.

Trajectories

I.

Crouched behind the wooded hill,
daylight levers dark,
pours down western trunks,
floods the hayfield hung with seed,
slides its amber lip
beneath the fog
and floats white mist
above the bearded weeds,
scooping up the night.

Why shouldn't women
carry away my heart perfectly
following the trajectories of seasons?

II.

Details, details, beauty of things,
blackberries so ripe
they rot in silk,
the small motions,
sandal slipping off a heel,
heat rising from the bow
of neck beneath thick hair,
a tossing of the head,
the vertebrate, the scented sky.

That's how love begins, lying
back on currents in the green creek,
giving up to slip between black stones.

III.

Three billion women
on the earth and just this one,
this one, so many desires
for so short a life,
women swarming
to the cities,
swallows leaving,
taking their shadows with them,
I am surely dying.

Glimpses of their flight through leaves,
they overshoot these sacred mountains,
the bombardment circling away.

Coronary

The dog he
lifts his big warm head
off of my feet, one less comfort
in the rain that gutters in the can
and shakes the panicles
and fells the saturated bee.

Hummingbirds arrive
between the cells, I hear
the next one far away, I feel
the heel of thunder in my chest,
the wet road pale as cloud,
ten skies shining on my nails.

May I meet a sanguine god
who lacks a sense of irony
his breath a fog
upon the pane, a comfort
in the dripping dark, the rain
beads on his muzzle.

The Settled Life
(Congratulating Mary Karr)

Your footwear is outrageous,
heels as square and long as stakes
that pitch you forward though you stand
upright and stamping for a brawl,
only colleagues or the limned aristocrats
to bite, and they best watch their asses.

Already I can see you flinch,
the years in ordinary towns upstate,
the well bored deep and pumping,
your private hell best-sold,
the cross you hung
that pulses at your throat.

Pour salt around the fishhouse
where you once felt safe,
moist words sublime like arsenic
in common, unfamiliar light,
the continent rolled open where you passed,
a great future in your wake.

The Renderer Faces Surgery

Organs pumping heat over the beechwood handle
I push the blade through suet leaning
heavy on the knife, over the shank I trust
even though a hundred times I feel the sting of
        amputation,
blood the only vibrancy in middle January.

When the bullet enters just above the eye,
when the steer stops kicking,
hook the chain around his heels and hoist him upside
        down,
open up his heart and drain him, trust the blade and
        push,
trust the surgeon's ego and the abattoir's routine.

We are not so well constructed beyond bones,
suet hung behind the liver on weak rags,
how tidy it all seems,
vitals rolling out to melt the snow,
        the empty cage.

Smooth as marble I cut suet warm with reek,
I lean heavy on the blade,
half-a-ton of being off the hoof.
        I am less tender than the beeves,
but lack the proof.

Proof

Moon on the ground
after the icicle days
after the sugar snow
after the organ pipes
fall from the eaves
moon on the ground
after the feathers of hoarfrost
drop from the stems
after the wreckage of birds
after the voles and the thaw
moon on the ground
after the commonplace doubt
after the atman lies pooled
after the rain on the fields
moon on the ground
fragile and after and here.

Last Reading in Pittsburgh
(Upon hearing Maxine Kumin, Dec. 8, 1999)

There's no explaining horses,
it just happens,
shiver in the withers, eye of God
rolling white in panic,
800 pounds of terrified muscle
hauling the wagon over you.

She apologizes for losing her place,
shielding her eyes against the cataract
of odd brown light on stage,
wishing she could see, all those untamed
minds down in the dark smoldering
with singular magnificence,
sure of their *impunitas*,
safe in the university from iron shoes.

She reads another poem about bears,
a faint song, a ghost dance,
lucky to be alive or maybe not, she says,
stooped at the lectern, flipping the white pages
of her work selected, facing her profession,
lost again in the edited natural order of things,
more chaos barned than the brave can nurture,
dumb chance in every stall,
death without dimension.

Five-Point

He turns a finger in the entry wound,
up to the knuckle between the shoulder blades,
wide-eyed in war paint, my son,
tendons iced pink,
pink the hunters' sound for lung blood,
arrow opened auricle,
the clean quick kill, the old male skill.

Troopers found him in the trunk,
my brother's boy, front page news.

Clothesline tied around his neck and knees,
how easily he drags,
shoulder plows a trough that fills with sunset
pink, how heavily he lifts,
muscled flanks weigh down the lowered gate,
every life adrift across the buried road,
the wind reminding us this is the world.

My brother aged before my eyes,
the casket closed, pictures on a board.

Thirty feet up, dressed as a dormant oak,
my son invisible as faith
among the trees against the whetstone sky,
face smeared with pigments of the earth,
the arrow knocked, the ancient hearts
leaping in their native ground,
quivering and drawn.

Believers

Dying's a procession
so we stop,
deep in crystal sixes
fallen from the sky, afraid
the stump-legged dog
might burst his honest heart.
The storm drives on without us,
enfilades erase the wood,
wind sifts where we've been,
the volleys of the heart erupt without us,
the whole, round earth beneath us,
gravity and grace among us,
sure of that.

Resurrection

The presence of absent men
creates hollows at the table
for loops of women serving
casseroles with padded mitts
against the burn of ministry
in beautiful, primitive procession.

This year, the longest widowed
points a burled finger, and I
assume the chair before the window,
shoulders hot with afternoon
draped like linen across town
civilized by graves and dandelions.

Maples veil the empty streets,
inchworms chew new leaves,
women live too long,
lining up their pills beside their plates,
expecting men in me,
and I a weakling king unsure

Of everything except that I
am not the only one who hears
his father still alive.

NOTES

Epigraph from "The Wanderings of Oisin," by William Butler Yeats, 1889.

19 - The last two lines are from Chia Tao's (Middle T'ang) "Overnight at a Buddhist Mountain Temple."

20 - The last phrase is part of Emily Dickinson's "quaint and aphoristic" conversation with Thomas Higginson as recorded by him in his *Atlantic Monthly* essay. Of her remark, Higginson wrote it was "said very timidly and suggestively, as if they were meteors and comets."

27 - The spring of 1998 is remembered in the village of Scullton for two unprecedented events, an infestation of Asian ladybird beetles, and a tornado.

32 - *The New Yorker* is a tough nut to crack. In California, members of the Heaven's Gate cult committed mass suicide in 1997, hoping to free themselves from their bodies, board a ship they believed hidden behind Hale-Bopp, and ride to paradise.

36 - A brief but lively correspondence with a poet on the cover of the *American Poetry Review* ended when I guessed she had mistaken me for a better-known writer.

37 - Obscurity can be a compliment to the reader. Nevertheless, I offer the following: Pisces is the twelfth sign of the zodiac; "Greater Elegance" is a lift from a poem by Wei Feng (Sung dynasty); Ganoidei (a superorder) and Teleostei (a subclass) are primitive fish. I believe the last two lines to be Chinese, but cannot locate the reference. Tu Fu?

40 - D. B. Zimmerman was the richest man in his county before the Great Depression. His house is now a bed and breakfast surrounded by an outlet shopping mall.

41 - Edgar Speers was chairman of USSteel at a time of peak production at the Duquesne Works, site of this poem, in the Monongahela Valley. Of the mill that once employed 4,000 men, only a few outbuildings remain, and a heritage park.

43 - Ecclesiastes 10:19.

49 - As an experiment, little-known poems by three brilliant poets were submitted over a *nom de plume* to a respected literary magazine. All were rejected and returned in two weeks without comment.

59 - Mary Karr's autobiography, "The Liar's Club," has been a runaway best-seller. A sequel, with its substantial advance, may have already been released.

63 - In memory of Devin O'Brien, born July 19, 1976, shot to death in a Maine stone quarry April 25, 1997. The third stanza ends with a William Stafford line.

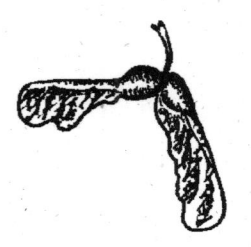

Jeff O'Brien writes in the Laurel Mountains eighty miles east of Pittsburgh and is happy to leave it at that.